Everyday Conversations with God

Judith A Green

First published by Busybird Publishing 2021

Copyright © 2021 Judith A Green

ISBN
Print: 978-1-922691-12-5

This work is copyright. Apart from any use permitted under the *Copyright Act 1968*, no part of this publication may be reproduced, stored in a retrieval system or transmitted in any form or by any means, electronic, mechanical, photocopying, recording or otherwise, without the prior written permission of Judith A Green.

Cover Image: Blaise van Hecke

Cover design: Busybird Publishing

Layout and typesetting: Busybird Publishing

Busybird Publishing
2/118 Para Road
Montmorency, Victoria
Australia 3094
www.busybird.com.au

*To Rev Paul Blacker
who gave me voice.*

*To the people of
Lilydale Uniting Church
who shared the journey.*

Introduction

God's voice is not confined to a special place. It is often clearest in places we do not expect to hear it, in the most ordinary moments of our everyday lives.

Several years ago, I was invited to write the front-page reflection for *Lighthouse*, the weekly newsletter of Lilydale Uniting Church. This small booklet is a compilation of fifty-two of those reflections, one for each week of the year.

As you read these reflections, I hope you too hear God's voice in the ordinary, everyday moments of your life.

I acknowledge the traditional custodians of the land on which I live and write and pay my respects to Elders, past, present and emerging.

Like A Creek After Rain

Wise God,

Sometimes, as I attempt to write these reflections, the ideas and words flow like a creek after rain. How good writing feels then.

There are days though, when it's like trudging through creek bed mud after a long hot summer, or on really bad days, the creek bed is dry. You know those times God when I implore you, 'Please help me'. You always do. An idea, a word, a story, a Biblical passage kick starts the thought process. I might fight with the words, but you guide their eventual shape.

As I hit the 'send' button, I also send you a heartfelt prayer of thanks for listening and answering, enabling me to fulfil my commitment. But I ask your forgiveness God for those easy weeks, when the ideas and words flow like a creek after rain, and I don't thank you. When I'm sure my efforts are solely mine. Like a child thinking they are grown up, and running off to play, I think I can do it alone. The same child, running back to a parent when it all gets a bit scary, just as I run back to you when the words won't come.

A wise parent, you never turn your back on me, forever present, hand outstretched, waiting for me to reach out to you. Forgive me God, for failing to remember your love forever flows like a creek after rain. How good it feels when I remember that, God. How good it feels, living in your love forever flowing like a creek after rain. It is then my thanks flow, not because of what you have done for me, but because you are who you are, my God.

Amen

Breath of God

It was an ideal gardening day, the clear blue sky a perfect backdrop to a golden globe sun. The leaves of the trees absolutely still, waiting, for the first breath of the day. In the stillness, it was almost as though the earth itself was holding its breath, waiting, for day's first breath.

The calm slowed my own breathing as it seemed to slow time itself, slowing my actions as I enjoyed the world of my own backyard without worrying about how many weeds I needed to deal with before the darkness of night ended my time in the garden.

When the breeze came it was just a whisper, a faint movement of the leaves, a gentle touch across the backs of my hands, the top of my head, as I was kneeling pulling up weeds. It passed through, yet never quite left, as the leaves maintained a gentle sway.

Spirit God, we look for you in the roaring winds, claps of thunder and bolts of lightning.

We search your Word, attempting to discern your message for today leading us into tomorrow from the stories of yesterday. We lift our eyes to the hills and search the valleys, we lose track of you sometimes in the death and destruction, the sense of hopelessness splashed across our daily newspapers. Then, in the most ordinary of moments, in the most ordinary of places, as I do a most ordinary task, you breathe upon me, remind me you are always there as you always have been, in every breath I take.

Amen

Let Us Sing for Joy

'Come, let us praise the Lord! Let us sing for joy to God, who protects us!
Let us come before him with thanksgiving and sing joyful songs of praise.' Ps 95: 1-2

Protector God,

Sometimes I come to worship with a thousand thoughts running relays in my head. I come, out of a sense of duty rather than a sense of worship. Outwardly, I display the 'right' attitude, you know my inner being. Yet, when the first notes of the introit are played the relays falter a little, and I'm glad I have come.

Thank you for words and music working in tandem. For hymns of yesteryear, hymns of today and shorter choruses. For the contemplative, the sombre, the joyous, the familiar and those I have yet to learn. I give thanks for the times you have given me a gentle shake during worship, reminding me to sing with my heart not only my mouth.

Thank you for the music, God. For the times it reflects how I feel and the times it soothes and calms, uplifts and inspires, challenges and urges a change of direction or thought. For when music is the prayer and the message, when you speak, and I listen.

Thank you for composers and hymn writers, for instrumentalists and singers, using their talent to share your message. You know something else God, I'm really glad I don't have to be a good singer to sing during worship, that you're happy with my voice just as it is, and I feel free and welcome to share in songs of worship with my fellow worshippers.

Amen

Journeying

There is a strong German influence in the Barossa Valley, Hahndorf and Tarrington. Burra and Moonta have a strong Cornish connection. Place names, street names, cultural festivals, architecture all reflect where these people came from. Looking back, we understand why the Germans and Cornish, along with other nationalities, in an unfamiliar land, needed to be with those of a common background, speaking the same language, sharing similar customs and faith. Who understood not only what they had come from, but the difficulties of the life in their new home. Looking back, we know these people are us. From our diverse backgrounds, we have become Australians.

Today, it seems, we are afraid of newcomers who establish their own communities – Vietnamese, Sudanese, Buddhists and Muslims. Yet, we look back with compassion on the Germans escaping religious persecution, the Cornish fleeing famine and poverty. Are today's migrants and refugees any different to the Germans and Cornish of our history books? Aren't many of those who seek refuge on our shores today also fleeing persecution, famine, and poverty? In our journey of becoming Australians have we forgotten the poverty many of the indigenous people endure, as we celebrate 'our' national identity.

Loving God, forgive me, not only the times I've failed the Good Samaritan test but failed to accept I'm the one lying beside the road in need of care. In failing to acknowledge my own wounds, I've also failed to accept a stranger's gracious gift of healing, in the binding of my wounds. In failing to accept my own humanness I've closed my eyes to the common humanness connecting a diverse people. Forgive me gracious God.

Amen

A Reflection on The Start of a New School Year

A new school year has to be worn in just as a new pair of school shoes has to be worn in. Initially, new shoes and wearer's feet are not comfortable with one another. The shoes may cause blisters until they soften a little, accepting the wearer's unique walking style. Likewise, feet object to conforming to well-supported shoes, particularly if they have been unconfined all summer, flip flopping around in thongs.

It may be the start of a new school year, but students, teachers and parents still carry last year's baggage. The baggage may be light and supportive if the previous year was a positive experience. It may weigh heavy, distorting their perspective if the previous year was filled with struggle and perceived failure.

Teacher God, open our ears to all those starting the new school year. Help us to hear their words, their tone of voice, to listen to their stories. Open our eyes to the way they walk, the way they approach and talk to others. Open our hearts to what they are *not* saying, to changes in behaviour or attitude and how last year's experiences may be affecting their resilience.

Remind us each school is part of the community in which we live. The experiences of students, teachers and parents are interactive with the wider community. May our words be the light and supportive baggage each takes with them into the new school year, may our actions soothe blistered feet until new shoes and wearer's feet are comfortable with one another. Help us to discern when blisters are caused by more than new school year discomfort.

Amen

Not Perfect Yet Still Splendid

Several years ago, I was given a camellia. I planted it and being drought time, watered it consistently. It grew, sprouting lush green leaves and splendid flowers. The drought ended. Heavy rains became a deluge.

The organisation further up the slope from where we live had altered the water course when they established an oval. The drainage channels set up to stop excessive water running through our properties had not been maintained during drought time. It sounded as though we had a river running under our house. Our plants, especially the camellia, suffered. It stopped growing, developing a fungus on its leaves. I was about to dig it up one day when I noticed some buds appearing on the now almost bare branches and new fungus-free leaves sprouting. Rather than dig it up we cut off all the affected leaves and pruned the dead sections from the branches. The new leaves shone as camellia leaves do and the flowers were as splendid as they had always been.

The deluge has stunted the camellia's growth. It has healthy leaves, although it isn't what I'd call a beautiful specimen of a camellia. Yet despite its limitations, it flowers profusely, adding colour to our garden and giving us much pleasure.

Creator God, sometimes I allow yesterday's scars to stunt who I am. Yet, if I lay them at your feet, my scars become my strength. Despite my limitations you do not discard me, you have a purpose for me in the world in which we live. Despite my limitations you set me on the path to live your Word and walk with me.

Amen

Harvest Thanksgiving

The ears of wheat were central to the table on Harvest Thanksgiving Sunday in the Church I grew up in. Even in drought years, when harvest yields were vastly diminished, Harvest Thanksgiving was celebrated, as it still is, in many rural communities today.

Perhaps it is the farmer's daughter in me, but I miss Harvest Thanksgiving Sunday, the earthy reminder of sowing and reaping. But the grains of wheat were also a symbol of what we sow and reap in our lives. Being thankful for and willingly sharing not only a bountiful harvest but continuing to do so in drought times. Giving thanks not only for the community in which we live, but those who have gone before us. The seed they have sown is our harvest, as the seeds we sow will be our children's harvest.

Part of our offering at Church each Sunday is the practical gifts for those in need within our community, for those who have a diminished or no crop to reap. Rather like a weekly mini-Harvest Thanksgiving.

Harvest Thanksgiving was a time of giving thanks for what we have received and our ability to give to others. More importantly however, it was a time to praise God for His enduring presence, not only when the harvest is bountiful, but the gift of hope God gives to sustain us, even when the rains do not fall.

Sustaining God, when we give to others, may we give in the spirit of hope, you have given so freely to us.

Amen

A Shrove Tuesday Prayer

My Saviour God.

How I delight in the taste sensations of pancakes, the butter and lemon juice, jams and creams, cinnamon and fruit and other delectable morsels dribbling down my chin and fingers. How I devour and savour the flavours and smells and reach for another and another, smothering each in a variety of toppings, until I finally sit back, my appetite sated.

Shrove Tuesday is such fun. But what about Ash Wednesday? Still filled with the food delights of the previous day will I be ready to listen for the rumblings and rumours of those plotting your death. Clinging to the joy of sharing a feast, will I ignore the smell of mob mentality? In the cleaning up of the dregs of pancake mixture will I also attempt to erase the intense fear and dread your followers were experiencing?

Seated at a laden table giving thanks 'for what I am about to receive', do I recall the family in the next street, their table sparsely set, or the members of your family in distant lands their skeletal frames barely breathing?

Forgive me Lord for the ease with which I give thanks for my abundance as I pray eloquently for those who have so little, then think my job is done. Forgive me my inaction. Open my heart to your message, 'whatever you did not do for the least of these you did not do for me'. Remind me, that despite my many weaknesses your love still embraces me, and only in your wisdom and understanding will I find the empathy to act.

Amen

A Woman Of Faith

Nearly thirty years ago, on a busy inner-city street, as our three-year-old son studied a bug on a tree, a very frail, elderly nun stopped for a chat.

'When I was young,' she told me, 'I loved swimming. But nuns weren't allowed to swim then. Now we are. But my doctor won't let me.' She didn't wait for sympathy. 'When I get to heaven,' her eyes sparkling, 'there will be a swimming pool there.' She continued, 'They tell me God keeps us on this earth until our work is complete. I'm not sure what it is I still have to do, and this worries me, because I don't think I've got much time left.'

While some of the warmth came from the autumn sun it was the richness of the woman's faith I found inspiring. In obviously frail health she wasn't waiting to die, she was still striving, still searching to serve God in whatever way He asked of her, willingly and graciously, until her final breath. That very same God, well, he'd understand about the swimming as well. What a wonderful relationship she had with her God.

I would never presume to know God's plans for this lovely lady, but the calmness and peace she left me with, her gentle sharing of a living faith, of a God who knew her and loved her, whom she desired to serve, inspires me still. I always think of her as a woman of faith, not because she was a nun, not because of what she said, but because the simple joy of life, the love of God for her and her love for God, was as though a sunbeam was growing inside her.

Philippians 3: 4b-14

The Good Fruit

Many years ago, in the Church I attended at that time, there was a wise, gracious, caring woman. She had the ability to speak the truth in a difficult situation which encouraged discussion, not conflict, her words opening the way for reconciliation, rather than animosity. I admired her integrity immensely.

One day, she shared an incident which occurred in the early days of her husband's ministry. In their congregation was an annoying and extremely outspoken woman. It became too much for this now gracious lady and she spoke her mind to this woman in a very ungracious manner. She remembered the hurt her words caused many decades later, as though it was that day.

Loving God, we thank you for the faithful who inspire us. Their inspiration is not in what we perceive as human perfection, but in their imperfections, which mirror our own. In revealing their imperfections, they reveal the power of your love. For, despite imperfections, when we walk in your love, you work through us, to bear the good fruit.

Amen

A Prayer for This Moment

God of my every moment, between the inhaling and exhaling of this breath I kneel before you.

For all the breaths I have taken while experiencing the warmth of the sun or refreshing rain, the glory of sunrises and sunsets, laughter and tears, I thank you. For friends and strangers who guided me on paths lush with soft grasses and perfumed flowers and those paths littered with deep potholes, I thank you.

For the unknown number of breaths, I have yet to take I thank you. For places you will lead me and challenges you will set before me. I may not like all of these as I have not always liked what you asked of me in the past. I've grumbled, complained, ignored your calls, shouted, and whimpered, 'not I Lord, not I'. But in your graciousness, you patiently wait until I kneel before you, reach out to you, allowing myself to inhale and exhale in the pattern you designed specifically for me before I breathed my first breath.

For this very breath I am now taking I thank you. Just as you know when even a sparrow falls you are aware of every single breath I take. When fear and anxiety shorten my breaths, when pain is a gasping breath, when joy a golden breath you know.

God of my every moment, between the inhaling and exhaling of this breath I kneel before you, lay the path of my living at your feet, walk assuredly with you as you lead me one breath at a time.

Amen

The Lesson I Learnt from Goop

Sometimes change is a bit like jumping from a plane. We are heading for the ground at a rapid rate of knots until we remember we are wearing a parachute and pull the rip cord.

I felt like this when I resigned from teaching. I had a new path to follow but the jump was scary. The parachute I relied on was life lessons I learnt from the children.

When the challenge I have set myself seems too hard I recall the Goop, also known as Goo or Slime, I offered the children. Some loved it, others walked away fast, some felt with one finger, then wandered away to return later and try again.

When I am tempted to turn my back on my new career, I hear an echo of my words to the children, 'Give it a go. You don't know what it feels like until you try it.' The sheer delight on the faces of those who were initially hesitant, when they found the courage to plunge their hands and arms into the Goop, is something I treasure.

The children learnt more than the properties of Goop however. They conquered their fear of the unknown and took a chance.

The unknown is always there. It is our choice to ignore or explore. To stay safe or to jump and trust the parachute we are wearing.

A Reflection on Psalm 32

The days of the week and the months of the year follow a familiar pattern, as do the Liturgical seasons. There's security in following a familiar pattern. Security in knowing God is ever present. Yet, I can take God's presence for granted, as in the times I assume God will forgive my wrongdoing and I bypass the need to ask for forgiveness.

As a child I knew I was loved, despite my disobedience. But my disobedience was never brushed under the carpet. It was in those moments when I was honest with myself and admitted my wrongdoing I felt the depth of my parents' love for me in their forgiveness.

Forgiving God, as your child, I know I am loved, despite my disobedience. But You do not control me 'like a horse or a mule, which must be controlled with a bit and bridle to make it submit'. It is in those moments when I am honest with myself and confess my sins to You, I feel the depth of Your love for me in Your forgiveness.

Freed from my wrongdoings, I submit to Your ever-present protective security, for it is in such obedience I experience the God-based happiness which makes me 'shout with joy!'

Amen

The Soft Whisper Of A Voice
(1 Kings 19:12b)

The air seemed full of invisible droplets of ice, as I climbed the old poppet head tower, on the summit of Mt Tarrengower outside Maldon. I wasn't free to soar as an eagle soars but was enthralled by the picture perfect 360-degree view. But a more powerful sensation was the silent stillness, a sense of calm, quiet and peace, beyond the noise of busyness.

When busyness is my burden, when peace and calm evade me, I often recall the silent stillness of Mt Tarrengower. As the calm essence of that experience fills me, I sense God's presence. As I make time to be with God, I feel the burden of my busyness lighten.

God of 'the soft whisper of a voice', I yearn to sit in your presence, but am distracted by tasks needing to be done. 'I'll complete the tasks first then I won't be distracted when I sit in your presence,' I tell myself. Then I come to you, weary from my busyness.

God of 'the soft whisper of a voice', when I come to you, at the dawn of each new day, kneel at your feet and listen to 'the soft whisper of a voice', busyness is no longer my burden. Peace and calm do not evade me, for when my day begins in your presence, you walk with me in my busyness. My tasks do not need to be completed to sit in your presence, because you, God, of 'the soft whisper of a voice' are the silent stillness sustaining me through the day.

Amen

An Easter Prayer

Loving God, from my safe perspective in a land where I am free to worship you, it is almost impossible to imagine the political and social climate of that first Easter. I've judged Peter for his denials, Mary for failing to recognise you at the open tomb and Thomas who doubted, until he saw Christ's wounds for himself.

Open my eyes to the harsh reality of those days and weeks culminating in Christ's death and resurrection. Open my eyes to the harsh reality of my own denials, of failing to recognise you and doubting until I see you for myself. It is much easier to judge another than admit my own weaknesses. Guide me amidst the crowd hungry for blood and death, along the path of sorrow in the garden to the confusion of an empty tomb, stand beside me as I share Thomas' doubts. Awaken in me the raw grief of Christ's followers, their despair and fear, then joy and wonder at the mystery and perplexity of resurrection.

Over two thousand years has silenced the roar 'Crucify him', stilled the dust of countless feet watching Christ stumble as he carried the cross. It has masked the stench of death and fear, the stories of faithful disciples in the years following the resurrection of Christ. It has taken the sting from their confusion and their deepest despair.

Open my eyes, eternal God, to those I can see and those in faraway places, the hungry and thirsty, the homeless, those cowering in fear in war zones or harsh regimes. Walk with me beyond Easter to live the love and hope of Christ's death and resurrection.

Amen

The Healing Power of Touch

In recent years I have been a frequent visitor to hospitals and an aged care facility. During these many visits I have observed and experienced the immensely healing power of touch.

Staff stroking the hand of an agitated, dementia-lost resident; sometimes words are spoken, sometimes they sit in silence. The agitation lessens as the resident is led by the hand to a place where they feel comfortable, often to another staff member who likewise uses touch to settle the person.

During an anxious time with a loved one in hospital recently, a very kind and caring nurse grasped the patient's hand firmly, listening intently, until his grasp relaxed, releasing her hand. As she left the room, she placed her hand gently on my shoulder, as the staff in the aged care facility I visit frequently do, during stressful times.

The healing power of touch does not come in a wand-like magical cure, an instant resolution, or a clearing of the rubble from the road I am on. It comes in a gentle acknowledgement the rocky road is real and long, but with the assurance I do not journey alone. The touch does not leave when the person lifts their hand, for the healing power of their touch is in the little of themselves they leave, as though they are walking with me.

Loving, protector God, I know you walk with me in every breath I take, yet there are times I struggle to sense your presence. Thank you, for your healing power of touch delivered by those you send to guide me past the boulders in my path. I sense your presence in their touch.

Amen

Sing A New Song

'Sing a new song to the Lord!
Sing to the Lord, all the world!' Psalm 96:1

The early morning dew was still fresh on the grass when our then-four-year-old grandson squatted down to watch a snail traversing our lawn. With his head twisted to one side he appeared to be trying to see underneath the snail. Eventually, he very gently lifted the snail off the ground and turned it over to watch the constantly moving underbelly. Surprisingly, the snail didn't withdraw into its shell, though the antennae were waving wildly.

He studied this slimy, endlessly moving flesh for some time, his fingers grasping the shell firmly without harming the creature. Finally, no doubt to the snail's relief, he placed it very gently back on the ground watching it continue its journey.

Creator God, thank you for the opportunity to view the world through a child's eyes, they see the familiar, anew. For the gentleness and innocence of a small boy, marvelling at and respecting one of your creations, untainted by adult perceptions of the snail as a plant devouring nuisance. Thank you, for stilling my tongue, enabling me to hear a new song in the silent trust of a snail in the hand of a small boy, and a small boy's wonder in the world around him.

Amen

A 23rd Psalm Reflection

When I was young, I had a pet rooster called Limpy, for obvious reasons. He could get around, but the 'law of the jungle' is survival of the fittest. He had his own shed. With personal feeding and care he lived a protected and comfortable existence. Being a rooster, he did not lay eggs. Being a pet, he did not end his days in the cooking pot but nor was he safe from the other chooks to be allowed out to enjoy fatherhood. In other words, he contributed little, to neither the chook kingdom nor the economy of the farm. Nevertheless, I loved him just as he was.

Shepherd God, sometimes I'm like Limpy, cowered down in the dust, contributing little and believing even less that I have anything to contribute. But, in your wisdom you inspired a writer to pen word pictures, lifting me from the dust of despair to rest amidst green pastures, walking beside still waters. The word images a reminder you accompany me through dark and light, protecting me from evil and comforting me, feeding me in abundance in the presence of my enemies, anointing my head with oil. These are not rewards for my achievements or my contributions, nor promises for future good deeds. None of this have I earned, nor expected to earn. Your goodness and mercy freely given, not only for today but all my days. However insignificant or weak I may feel, you lift me from the dust I am cowering in, because you love me, just as I am. My cup runneth over Shepherd God, with your love. You have restored my soul. I will dwell in your house, for evermore.

Amen

A Mother's Day Reflection

In my early years on the farm, a wood stove warmed our kitchen, kept the kettle boiling, scones and roasts cooked in its oven, and we made the most delectable toast no electric toaster will ever be able to produce. When the paddocks were white with frost, Mum and Dad would get up early, stoke the fire and place our clothes in the food warmer at the base of the stove. My brother and I would then race from our bedrooms into the by then warm kitchen, and hurriedly dress into luxuriously warm garments.

As a child, I assumed my world of being wrapped in unconditional love and warm clothes was everyone's world. When I ventured beyond my child's world, words like Mum, Dad and home were an emotional security blanket I carried with me. It was in the reality of this grown-up world however, I discovered such words, for some, conjure up memories of sorrow and despair. Of night time's darkness rather than day time's light. Where choices of parent or child have caused almost irreparable damage, where families are separated, where loving words are rarely spoken or expressed in actions.

Loving God, as the world around me seems to be focused on the gloss of Mothers' Day I give thanks, not for warmed clothes, but the love these actions were wrapped in. Remind me to look beyond my comfort zone, to recognise in others the sorrow and bitterness burdening their lives. Relying on your wisdom, may I always attempt to wrap my actions in love, so the hurting may experience your healing grace in their lives. May I extend, in the ordinariness of my day, the richness of the love wrapped in my warmed clothes, as it was so freely given to me.

Amen

Little Boxes

Remember the song about 'little boxes'? The ones made from ticky tacky and they all look just the same. I sometimes think the retail marketing calendar is a series of little boxes. Christmas. New Year. Valentine's Day. Easter. Anzac Day. Mothers' Day. Christmas in July. Fathers' Day. Halloween. Sometimes the boxes are bigger when there are holidays attached. Each one, however, is brightly wrapped with ribbons and bows to attract my attention and my money and slotted into the appropriate time of the year.

There are times though, as I grumble about all this commercialism, when I get a distinctly uncomfortable feeling squirming around inside me.

Am I creating tidy rows of little boxes in the Christian calendar slotting the different images of Jesus into the appropriate time of the year? Advent. Christmas. Epiphany. Lent. Easter. Pentecost. Do I decorate the boxes in the correct colour and symbols, yet when the time has passed, I slot the box back into its row, ready for the next time?

Am I like the men on the road to Emmaus, who failed to recognise Jesus because they weren't expecting to see him? Am I so focused on the seasons of the Christian calendar I'm not expecting to hear God's voice between the seasons? Or am I hiding in my little boxes, hoping God won't see my quivering faith? Won't call me to walk an unknown path with him?

Is this distinctly uncomfortable feeling triggered by my safe little boxes or is it God lighting 'a fire burning inside' me, who, despite my quivering faith is releasing me from their confines and leading me to walk an unknown path with him?

'Praise the Lord.'

Contemplating Weeds

Weeding the garden recently I wondered who decided which plants were weeds. What criteria was used to decide what should be discarded and what was worthy of nurture?

The rose bears a beautiful flower but has sharp thorns. Sour grass is a weed yet has a delightful yellow flower. Blackberry bushes bear delicious fruit, yet most councils ban cultivation. Camellias bloom profusely yet have no perfume. I rather like kangaroo paw, but they provide safe harbor for snails.

When we first established our garden, we went to great effort to grow lawn. However living near a bush area, a multitude of weed seeds soon joined the lawn seeds. We gave up attempting a bowling-green-type lawn nurturing the green weeds instead. It was much tougher anyway for the football and cricket games our sons played with their mates in the backyard. It also meant an immense variety of birds enjoy our 'weed lawn', rich with gourmet delights for the bird population.

Do we as a society sometimes label people as we do plants? Which label does society place on asylum seekers, the mentally ill, the lonely elderly at home or in aged care, the student struggling to learn to read, the client of Centrelink who lacks the capacity to fill in a form? Which label does society place on the footballer with outstanding skills, the student who tops their year level, the suburb with the biggest houses? What criteria is used to decide who is worthy of nurture and who sets the criteria?

'Every one of us, then, will have to give an account of himself to God.' Romans 14:12

Cornerstones And Keystones

The church walls are held in place by ivy although the roof, front door and windows are gone. The entrance steps and internal floor are rocky rubble. As the render crumbles from the wall the skill of those who built the little stone church is obvious in the still solid cornerstones of the walls and keystones of the arched windows and doorway.

It's been many decades since the last worship service in this little church yet within the old walls I unexpectedly had an immense sense of God's presence. Not because it was once a church, but as I stood marvelling at the workmanship, I knew the walls would eventually crumble and join the other rocks scattering the floor. It was then I felt the strong sense of an infinite God reminding me although the cornerstones and keystones will crumble God's presence will never crumble.

Sometimes when I yearn for a sense of peace and calm, I recall that little church. Recall those few moments when I wasn't searching yet felt such a strong presence of an infinite God. When I yearn for a sense of peace and calm, I know an ever-present God is waiting for my heart beats to welcome his presence.

'Praise the Lord, my soul! / Praise the Lord!' (Ps. 104:35b)

The Imperfect Bag

I enjoy patchwork and embroidery. About three years ago I bought a kit to make an appliqué bag. Two years ago I prepared the pattern pieces. About a month ago I finally put it together. Partway through, I realised I had placed a base piece on the top edge of the bag. It wasn't a major disaster. There is little difference between the two pieces. Neither the functionality nor the aesthetics of the bag was affected. But I knew the mistake was there.

Could I live with the imperfection, or should I unpick the mistake? I was about to commence unpicking, when I remembered the Amish women, (or perhaps God was nudging my memory), who always leave an imperfection in their beautiful quilts, as a reminder only God is perfect.

Sometimes we are so busy trying to be perfect, we actually work backwards. In focusing on, and searching for perfection, we fail to acknowledge imperfection is our humanness. A partially completed appliqué bag cannot fulfil its purpose, neither can we fulfil the purpose God has for us, if we are constantly working backwards, unpicking our mistakes, unwilling to take the risk of imperfection, rather than trusting in God's plan for us.

Perfect God, what a joy it is to be loved despite my imperfections. What a hope to share with others, they too are loved, despite their imperfections. What a wonderful assurance it is knowing even when I 'muck up' you still work through my imperfections to fulfil your purpose.

Amen

Rock Of Ages

Since its geological birth, Mt Sturgeon at the southern end of the Grampians, has experienced the dust storms of droughts, worn shrouds of fog, glistened in torrents of rain, been shadowed in hot summer sun, and pounded by gale force winds and hail bearing storms. Yet the ancient rocky Mt Sturgeon with its many cracks, crevices, indentations and furrowed stream-like erosions has withstood the battering of the elements for thousands of years and will stand for thousands of years to come. Today it overlooks lush green paddocks dotted with hundreds of grazing sheep in late winter into spring.

God of Strength, I thank you for the tangible timeless examples of your world which help me to understand the mysteries of who you are. Yet the more I think I understand the more I realise I don't understand, for your timelessness cannot be confined as the timeless strength of a rock is confined. Your strength is infinite and indestructible.

God of Gentleness, you are my rock, but unlike the ancient rocky surface of Mt Sturgeon your strength is wrapped in the gentleness of your love. The infinite magnitude of your strength and the all-encompassing embrace of your love, despite my human frailties, is far beyond my human understanding.

Ageless God, when Mt Sturgeon is long gone you will still be, just as you were, before Mt Sturgeon ever existed. I gaze at Mt Sturgeon and marvel at its geological birth when I should be marvelling at the One who created it. 'Rock of Ages, cleft for me/let me hide myself in thee.'

Amen

A Decrepit Car and Ragged Young Men

Many years ago, travelling the back way from Lilydale to Wonga Park late on a cold winter's night I hit a wombat. I couldn't leave the badly injured creature but none of the passing cars would stop. Eventually a young woman rushing to work stopped, promising to ring the police when she arrived. As I waited, two raggedly dressed young men in a decrepit car stopped. Somewhat alarmed, I stayed safely in my locked car, the window wound partly down. 'Are you okay?' they asked. I explained about the wombat, emphasising the police were on their way. 'What about your car?' They immediately knelt in the mud, checking the front of my car. I was perturbed by knocking and muttered voices. 'It's a bit dented, but nothing to worry about.' I thanked them repeating the police were on their way. 'Are you sure you're okay? We've been working on the car and came out to give it a run. We'll be in trouble with Mum if we don't get home soon.' I wound the window fully down then, ashamed of my initial judgment.

The next morning I told my then teenage sons about the young men. Their honest retort, 'and *you're* the one always telling *us* not to judge a book by its cover!' was justified.

Wise and loving God, you used a young woman in a rush and two raggedly dressed young men, to remind me about judging others by outward appearances. Through the brutal honesty only teenage sons can administer you reminded me I am still your child with much to learn. I prayed for safekeeping in the dark of that night. But you, wise and loving Parent God, kept me safe far beyond the physical comfort I asked for.

Amen

God's Children

When I was a child, I wasn't afraid of the dark, but I was afraid of the monsters which came out in the darkness. I could rationalise the snarling, thumping possum fights on our tin roof and go back to sleep. I could not rationalise the monsters of my imagination. Mum assured me the monsters wouldn't get into the house, but if by some chance they did sneak in, she would hit them with the frying pan. Mum's assurance didn't make the monsters go away, they were still out there somewhere, her assurance was she would keep me safe even if the monsters got inside the house.

As an adult it is such a joy and blessed assurance to be cocooned in God's parental love, to be called one of God's children. God's assurance doesn't keep the tough times away, doesn't mean no grief or sorrow in my life, God's assurance is his presence when the bad happens.

Parent God, I give thanks for the love my parents gave me so freely. In being loved as I was by my parents, I can embrace the concept of being one of your children, of being loved and feeling safe whatever may happen to me. Not everyone has had the positive experience of parents I have had. Walk with me Parent God, so I may choose my words thoughtfully, may act in a way that assures those I meet of your love, that your love will heal sorrows and hurts and keep them safe in a way human assurance cannot.

'When I lie down, I go to sleep in peace; you alone, O Lord, keep me perfectly safe.' (Ps 4:8)

Amen

Educating The Teacher

She'd lose the notes I'd sent home. Forget to pay excursion money when it was due. Chattered non-stop and asked the most annoying questions well after everyone else had left.

It was early in my teaching career. My assistant, several years older than me, reminded me how quickly the previous teacher managed to 'get rid of parents' at the end of a session. 'Help me God,' I remember pleading, as another session ended and 'the' mother headed in my direction yet again, my assistant glaring.

'Listen to my words, O Lord/and hear my sighs'. (Ps. 5:1)

God not only heard my words but my sighs, the emotions wrapped around the words. This time, as the young mum's annoying questions bombarded my ears I listened for her sighs, the emotions wrapped around her words. In doing so, I not only recognised the ploys those with low literacy skills use to survive in a literate world, but how easy it is to exclude when I view a situation from only my perspective.

Wise God, you peeled away my annoyance to reveal another's pain, exposing my potential to inflict further pain as I focused on keeping the peace rather than discerning the needs of the young mum. Thank you, for not only listening to my words and hearing my sighs, but educating me to listen to others, to hear their sighs, and for the strength and courage you instil in me to act. I'm still learning Teacher God. To you I offer praise and thanks for your patience.

Amen

A Hug from God

It's winter. The black clouds yet to shed their load are sinking earthward, masking the flimsy rays of a wintry sun as they do so. It appears late afternoon, yet the clock says 1pm. I'm sharing the kindergarten room with twenty-five, four and five-year-olds. We are cocooned in the encroaching cloud cover and the anticipated deluge which will keep us indoors.

My radiotherapy treatment is finished and my chemotherapy soon to come to an end. Part-time working hours and a caring, supportive assistant has meant I've been able to continue teaching through this health challenge. But today, tiredness overwhelms me. The heaviness of the clouds, the skittishness of the children keen to indulge in outdoor play denied them in recent weeks, weighs me down. I sit on my 'teacher's chair' watching the children at play, watching the clock, it too weighed down by the heaviness, ticks more slowly. 'How,' I beg of

God, 'will I find the strength, energy and will power to make it to 4pm?'

I'm not actually 'sitting' on my 'teacher's chair', more an 'exhausted slump', mentally and emotionally searching for some hidden well of strength to drink from. The children are busy, able to deal with their own needs for the moment, although one boy hesitatingly approaches me. I look towards him. He stands close to me, without speaking. I too am silent, letting him take his time to initiate the conversation.

Suddenly, the words burst from him. 'I think you just need a great big hug'. He wraps his arms around me in the warmest, most generous giant bear hug I am ever likely to experience.

A Child's Voice

I was an observer at a Poetry Slam heat. Three quiet, primary-school-aged children amongst the audience. My teacher's eye noted the 'potential' of a restless fourth!

Poetry quizzes punctuated the evening. The first required audience members to add a line to a given first line. The 'potential' boy flapped both arms excitedly, the MC gave him voice, his response, free of adult poetic restraints, received a WOW. The other children given voice amongst adults, produced further childlike lines of simplicity, packing a punch.

Participants performed their own poetry. The maturity of the winning poem suggested a poet with greater life experience than the thirteen-year-old girl who won. Yet, in the presentation it was her voice, her words, her emotion that captured us.

In the most unexpected of places, I was reminded not only of Jesus gathering the children around Him, but His words, 'whoever does not receive the Kingdom of God like a child will never enter it'.

May my ears be open to listen for a child's voice, my mind open to the words a child says and my heart free of adult constraints to experience the WOW of a child's wisdom.

The Power of Listening

Some of the late afternoon casual staff at the aged care facility I visit regularly are senior secondary students. They check water jugs, take meal requests for residents who eat in their rooms and help set up and serve meals in the dining room. They are enthusiastic, cheerful and the residents delight in their presence. They are a breath of fresh air for visitors who may be finding the going a bit tough too!

One afternoon I heard a nurse ask one of these students, a young man, to walk a resident to the dining room. He immediately walked beside the slow, frail, slightly confused lady, slowing his steps to her pace. As he walked, I heard him say, 'How's that book going you were telling me about? Have you finished it yet?' He was looking at her as he spoke, she immediately looked up at him with such a joyous smile and started telling him about the ending of the book. I could hear them talking in the now slower walk to the dining room. Walking and talking at the same time can be difficult at a certain age. He just slowed his pace to match her, leaning close to catch her soft voice. Obviously, it was a continuation of a previous conversation. It was as if that time with her was the most important thing that young man had to do in his day.

Caring God, thank you for those who work with the 'invisible' of our society with an attitude of compassion and love, bringing a sense of joy into their lives through the simple act of taking the time to listen and walking at a pace making conversation possible.

Amen

Belief And Faith

Reading Genesis 15: 1-12, I am reminded of the difference between believing in and having faith in God.

Abram listens and believes in God. But, in his humanness lacks the faith to accept God's promises will be fulfilled, in God's time, asking his Lord instead for tangible proof.

In the darkest depths of the night when sleep claims us, when dreams and nightmares as real as the day we have just lived, submerge us in a world beyond our control, we are at our most vulnerable. As children, it wasn't belief that made us call out to our parents from the edge of a bad dream, it was an unshakeable faith they were there waiting for our call, making the darkest night a safe place.

It was no different for Abram who 'fell into a deep sleep, and fear and terror came over him'. At his most vulnerable, at his weakest, when, like a child, it was his unshakeable faith knowing his Lord was there, that 'the Lord made a covenant with Abram', (verse 18).

How easy it is to believe in God's tangible creations, the ruggedness of the Grampians, the starkness of the Nullarbor, the mighty Murray, the lushness of the Daintree. Yet how hard it is to step, in childlike faith, into the yet to be chartered pea soup fog of tomorrow, without asking our Lord for a detailed map.

In The Silence

It was on the cusp of sunrise as I was leaving the family farm, suddenly, the first faint wave of colour broke night's darkness. In that instant the world was completely silent. Night creatures already settled for their rest, day creatures yet to awaken. I was in awe of this magnificent silence as wave upon wave of deepening colour flooded the skies.

God is as much in the rushing footsteps on a busy city street as in the silence of solitude. But sometimes, just as I need my nightly sleep, just as I need food to nourish my body, I need to step back from activity to feel again that sense of beauty and wonder. Not to turn my back on the world but to be still, wrapped in awe of the perfect silence of solitude, knowing God is restoring my breathing to a rhythm which will sustain me.

Infinite, loving God, you lead me beside still waters restoring my spirit in preparation for the path you have set before me.

Amen

Shoelaces

How long did it take to learn to tie your shoelaces? You probably watched a parent then tried and tried and tried again many, many times. How many times did you ask for help before finally mastering the shoelace tying technique?

Once you knew how to tie your laces, how long before you could tie your shoelaces firmly enough to keep your shoes on your feet?

It reminds me of my relationship with God. How many mistakes, (using insensitive words and excluding people, ignoring those in need, in too much of a hurry to listen to a friend beyond a brief 'hello', leaving tasks to that mythical 'someone else' to complete, saying an eloquent prayer for the starving, the homeless, the sick, the natural disaster victims yet by the time the prayer is finished I've forgotten all about them as I rush off in my very important busyness), will God keep forgiving?

I can tie my shoelaces without even thinking about it. But sometimes they come undone, tripping me up, my knees hitting the ground where my feet should be. As I retie my laces, more attentive this time, I recall not only the loving care of a patient parent teaching me to tie my laces correctly, but the loving care of a patient God, who, despite my endless and ongoing mistakes, is *still* teaching me the importance of praying diligently, so my shoes stay firmly on my feet.

Lessons Of War

My paternal grandma had two brothers and a cousin, who shared their home, killed in WWI. One of her brothers was at Queens College studying to be a Methodist Minister. I often wonder at the mental and emotional conflict he must have endured not only in his decision to enlist but the reality of battlefield killing. Grandma rarely mentioned these three young men. It was my dad who told me their stories and the effect of their loss on the family.

Yet despite the depth of their sorrow and loss, the family remained a family of faith. Their faith was expressed not only in regular worship attendance, not only in their active participation in the life of their worshipping community, but in the stories which have filtered through the decades. These stories are of loss and grief, not anger and bitterness. None of the stories are about 'the enemy' who killed the young men. None of hatred or dislike of the citizens of the countries these young men were fighting. They are stories of a family's love for those who died, of the loss and grief that comes from the death of loved ones.

Loving God, I thank you for those of faith who have gone before me, who in time of terrible loss and grief continued to live in your strength and love, who left behind stories perpetuating the power of your love to give strength to the sorrowing rather than focus on emotions which keep war alive long after the battles are over.

Loving God, guide us to open our hearts today to those around us suffering terrible loss and grief, may our words and actions not only acknowledge their pain but the power of your love to give them strength in their sorrow.

Amen

A Tiny Speck

Protector God,

You were with me on that country road I normally travelled in daylight. I was watching the time, vigilant about a consistent yet legal speed, while watching for kangaroos through an insect spattered windscreen. I rarely saw another car, just an occasional speck of light, a farmhouse with people unaware I was passing by, just as I was unaware of who they are.

The strangest thing, God, it was easier to feel your presence in nightlight than in daylight. In darkness, the sky and horizon become one, absorbing trees, fences, and buildings. I was a tiny speck on a massive black canvas just as farmhouses, car headlights, roadside markers and stars in the skies were all tiny bursts of light.

In the blackness however, I saw the power of light guiding me. I had no fear of the velvety soft darkness you wrap your world in as it rests, for you watch us as we sleep. The bursts of light, be they stars in the sky or of human creation, your guiding presence.

In the darkness, when I was just a tiny speck on this massive black canvas, I felt like it was just you and me, God. And it felt good.

Thank you, for reminding me however small I may feel, you not only know exactly where I am, but are all around me. Unlike daylight's horizon when sky and earth have a meeting place, night's horizon is never ending, but your loving presence, Protector God, extends far beyond even night times' never-ending horizon. How good it feels God, how very good indeed, knowing you surround me, a tiny speck on a massive black canvas, with a never-ending love.

> Amen

Celebrations

Traditionally kindergarten programmes have celebrated Father's Day, Mother's Day, Christmas and Easter. Today, kindergarten teachers are challenged regarding the validity of such celebrations.

One of the risks in celebrating Father's Day, for example, is it excludes those who follow a faith path which doesn't celebrate Father's Day. There is the added risk of distressing those who have lost their dad through death, or no longer live with or see their dad or have suffered an abusive one. Rather than risk excluding some, many kindergarten teachers choose to ignore such celebrations.

For me, there is an immense risk in this neutralising of cultural and religious celebrations. To ignore Father's Day is to deny the opportunity to share the joy and wonder of the father-child relationship. It also denies those suffering grief, hurt and bitterness the opportunity to have these emotions acknowledged and dealt with. It is an opportunity lost to share differences of faith and talking about ways to work with the difference.

Eliminating cultural and religious celebrations may eliminate the risk of exclusion. But by doing so, we eliminate the opportunities to develop stronger relationships, as we recognise the varying emotional responses those around us have at these times. We eliminate the opportunities to open communication with those of varying beliefs and creating together an environment which includes the differences. By failing to take risks we have missed opportunities.

A Father's Day Reflection

As the junk mail in our letterbox shouts, 'Buy me. Buy me. It's Father's Day', I remember a warm and sunny day when I was about five years old. We lived in the town at the time. My dad was share farming, although he owned some land close to the property he and Mum would soon buy. The day I remember, just Dad and I went out to this land taking our lunch with us. I had beetroot sandwiches. I can't remember what we did, but I was spending the day with my dad and my beetroot sandwiches had never tasted so good.

Fast forward twelve years. Dad put L plates on the car. I was still at school and aiming for tertiary study. As I would have insufficient money in the foreseeable future to buy a car, I saw little sense in learning to drive. 'No daughter of mine,' Dad informed me, 'is going to be reliant on other people to get around.' I learnt to drive. Often the passenger when

I visit him now, Dad is 'still' teaching me to drive!

Loving God, today is Fathers' Day. Not everyone will be giving thanks for their dad, as I am for mine. Not everyone grew up in a home filled with warmth and caring, with a dad who guided with compassion and understanding. Remind me to be aware of those whose memories are filled with sorrow and bitterness. Clothe me in your wisdom. Guide me to wrap my words and actions in your love, so those who are hurting may experience your healing grace. May I extend, to those I meet, the richness of the love which flavours beetroot sandwiches and driving lessons, as freely as it is given to me.

Amen

Following The Rules

Recently I read a fiction story set in the 1200s titled *The Anchoress*. It is based on fact, however, of women who chose a life of constant prayer and contemplation. An Anchoress was permanently sealed in a very small cell with two small, curtained openings for communication and the passing of life and faith sustaining items inwards and outwards. They lived according to very strict rules set down in a book, 'Rule of Life'.

The only men an Anchoress could talk to were her priest and confessor. Two female maids tended her needs controlling the number of women who could visit for advice and prayer.

One of the openings was into the Church. One night a leper journeying to a leper colony, begged the Anchoress for food, as he had no money. She refused him and sent him away empty-handed, because she wasn't allowed to talk to men, although she had food in her cell she could have passed through the opening. One of the young priests broke the rule about lepers in Church allowing the man to stay the night as long as he was gone by first mass in the morning. He gave the leper food and his own cloak to keep him warm.

The Anchoress heard all this. She agonised and struggled with her love for God, her seclusion from the world, and her need to adhere so rigidly to the Rules she was denying herself opportunities to love her fellow human beings.

Loving God, teach me to live my life not by rules but in the spirit of your love. In loving freely as you love me, the rules will be fulfilled, not because I followed them but because of your love guiding my living.

Amen

Green And Gold

I gazed 'in awesome wonder' at the brilliance of green and gold. Winter rains had nourished abundant roadside grasses, new shoots on trees and planted crops. But the gold overwhelmed me. Canola, wattles in full bloom and sour grass bobbing in the breeze.

I gave thanks for this beauty, when only months before I despaired at the desolation of drought. Gave thanks for wattles and sour grass which, without any human intervention, survives, for frogs and birds with their innate survival instincts.

In my humanness, I do not understand drought and flood, hurricanes and earthquakes, nor explain how trees and weeds, birds and frogs learnt to survive a drought. But in the sight before me, I witnessed the power of God.

This power wasn't in the beauty. It was in the realisation that all I saw before me, although unseen, had been present during drought, seeds biding their time, frogs hibernating, birds migrating, trees with their roots deep in the earth. Where I had seen desolation, God's hand had already equipped plants and animals for survival.

I give thanks for a God who recognises my humanness. Who provides, through the visible, a reminder, that even in the most desolate of times, God's hand is at work, through the invisible. A reminder faith itself, is belief in the unseen, God's inexplicable, everlasting presence.

Two Umbrellas and Four Horses

During one of my country trips I was following directly behind a slow moving, large wheeled conveyance of some sort on a very straight stretch of road. I had no side view to work out what it was, but the two golf sized umbrellas offered passengers exposed to the elements little protection from the rapidly building black clouds. Passing, I was surprised to see it was an uncovered wagon drawn by four magnificent Clydesdales, the banner flapping on the back reading 'Wimmera Mallee Pioneer Museum Jeparit'.

Dad was with me. He immediately told me the walking pace of the horses and the walking pace of a man. He then worked out how many 'miles' the horses could do in a day and how long it would take to reach Jeparit. He wondered where the horses would be rested for the night, and who would supply their feed and water. I learnt a lot in a very short period of time, of life in another era.

Wise God, how often do I rush past these brief, unexpected moments considering them unimportant, focusing instead on my destination? How often do I fail to recognise the colour and texture they add to the journey, the warmth to a relationship? In considering my busyness more important, I undervalue not only the moment but the people of the moment. In rushing past I miss opportunities to experience something new, different, a challenge, a joy, a sorrow or a lingering moment of wonder.

How often have I missed the side road you were beckoning me down, on the journey you have planned for me?

Amen

He Restoreth My Soul

In her book, *Celtic Treasure – unearthing the Riches of Celtic Spirituality,* Liz Babbs talks of the Celtic Saints who chose to live in or visit remote natural places who, 'believed that the veil between heaven and earth was 'thin' in these holy places and so it was easier to sense God's presence there.'

I may not be in a remote natural place, when I read Psalm 23, but the use of first-person pronouns of this Psalm, especially when I read the King James Version with its poetic expression and language, I experience a sense of solitude, a sense of being alone with God. In my often-busy world, times of solitude, of being alone with God, are times of soothing calm, of healing, of listening, of focusing not on the world around me but on my relationship with God

Shepherd God, you are my solace, my strength, my comforter, and my protector. When my busyness hides you from me you lead me to a 'thin' place of green pastures and still waters, of solitude and time alone with you, my gracious, loving God. When I return to my busyness, for actions are part of fulfilling your purpose for me, I carry your presence with me, for you, Shepherd God, hath 'restoreth my soul'.

Amen

Faith And Praise

Ever have one of those days when your feet and heart seem filled with lead? When physical activity is a monumental effort, when prayer is a chore rather than a joyous communion with God? When you do pray you deliver a list of problems you don't know how to resolve rather than give thanks and praise. 'Oh ye of little faith,' I often mutter to myself on such days.

Yet on those days wondering where my faith is, wondering why I find it so difficult to praise God, I realise it isn't my faith that is weak but my humanness. When burdens are too great, I crumple at the feet of God rather than kneel but whatever my posture I am always at the feet of God. If words of praise seem difficult to find, if prayer a chore rather than a joy, it is that praise has taken on a different colour that day. I may be physically weak but through my faith I know the only way for the burden to be lifted is to trust in God's wisdom and love.

God of wonder and mystery, I praise you for your goodness, your never-failing strength, your almighty power, and your wisdom. When I am at my weakest wondering where you are, you haven't left me, you are there where you always are. In my crumpled state as I rest on your feet, I feel the warmth of your love. When my weakness has left me feeling insignificant and unworthy you give me the strength to rise from my crumpledness to kneel before you. It is then I truly recognise your wonder and mystery, your truth and power and joyfully exclaim 'my God, how great thou art'.

Praise be to God.

Amen

Unexpected Wonder

When I was teaching, I often had a wildlife incursion for the children where they learnt about and touched snakes, lizards, crocodiles (mouth taped closed!), frogs, birds and tortoises amongst other Australian creatures.

One of the snakes was a half-grown python. I have a healthy respect mixed with a life-preserving degree of fear of slithering creatures. However, I managed to overcome my fear as the python was draped around my neck. It was incredible feeling its strength as it curled around my neck while balancing on my shoulders. I understood how easily a python strangles its prey.

What surprised me more than anything, was the delicate softness of the skin. Growing up on a farm I'd seen plenty of snakes, but touching was forbidden! Discarded snake skins were dry and crispy by the time we found them. The smooth, soft and gentle skin of a live snake, however, is an exquisite delight, not unlike the delicate skin of a newborn babe. The look of wonder on the children's faces when they found the courage to touch these snakes was a further delight. They too had not expected such delicate softness.

Creator God, I marvel at the physical world you created, sunrise and sunset, black skies pierced by lightning, soaring eagles and fluttering butterflies, mighty elephants and minute spiders, roaring lions and quilled echidnas, armadillos and giraffes, pelicans and willy wag tails. Yet, there are times I shroud your creations, the tangible and intangible, in my fear, denying myself the opportunity to marvel at the unexpected, denying myself the anticipation and expectation of the revelation of the unknown, denying myself the opportunity to respond in joyous wonder, 'Praise the Lord'.

Amen

Shalom

The title of Tolstoy's *War and Peace* probably expresses the common perception of peace as being the opposite to, or absence of war. The peace, Christ's peace however, which we pass during worship is not the peace of *War and Peace*.

'The peace that Christ gives is to guide you in the decisions you make; for it is to this peace that God has called you together in one body. And be thankful.' (Col. 3:15)

Christ's peace is a belonging. It is not an absence, as in the absence of war in worldly peace, but a completeness, a unity, a oneness.

If I stub my toe, my whole body is aware of my pain. If I cradle a newborn child, my whole body is aware of my joy. So it is, in being called to one body, any thought I have or action I take, is felt by all parts of the body.

When I speak the words, 'the peace of the Lord be with you', it isn't just my tongue speaking, it is the joining of hands and the connection of the eyes as I hear the response, 'and also with you'. The giving and receiving of Christ's peace is not only our acknowledgement of our oneness with Christ, but our commitment to work as one. Just as each part of our human body serves a different purpose, so each of us as part of one body serves a different purpose.

Loving God, we give thanks for our individuality. For it is our individuality that creates the different parts of the one body your peace calls us to be. We give thanks for your gift of peace, which is beyond human peace, a peace which binds and unites, yet sets us free. 'And we are thankful.'

Amen

A Tuesday Talk with God

It's Tuesday God. You know, the day before Wednesday, when I have to finish the *Lighthouse* front page. I've done the readings; let them percolate. Now I'm sitting in front of a blank computer screen. Sometimes it comes easy. You drop abundant hints and clues. Ideas flow, words fall into place, the front page takes shape, I press send well before Wednesday night's deadline.

Other times, like today, all I do is press delete, empty the page of mismatched words, or misshapen ideas. Am I not listening to you God? Am I so busy multi-tasking, your hints and clues jumble with everything else in my head? Or do I want a restaurant style serving, when I don't do any of the planning, preparation or cooking?

I want to write about mountain top experiences, God. The times I've sensed your presence in majestic mountains or the delicacy of a wildflower growing in a rock face wall. Instead, I'm sitting here on a very ordinary, non-mountain top experience sort of day, grumbling. And you're listening. I know you are. I'm not so good at listening. Well God, I do always listen. It's just sometimes, well, like today, I want to write about mountain top experiences, and you keep changing the subject, dropping hints and clues about ordinary days.

God of majesty and ordinary, sometimes your presence overwhelms me in a mountain top experience; I bow down in wonder and awe. In my ordinary days I take your presence for granted. Today, on a very ordinary, non-mountain top experience sort of day, I bow down in wonder and awe, for wherever I am, you are always there. God of majesty and ordinary, I bow down in wonder and awe, for wherever I am, you are always there.

Amen

Through A Child's Eyes

On a recent sunny afternoon, I spent time in a garden with a two-year-old. 'Dig. Dig.' I was instructed, a small plastic spade thrust into my hand. While clearing a section of weeds in readiness for our excavations I disturbed a garden spider and two small snails. The spider scurried for cover; the two snails began to slither up the colour bond fence.

Most gardeners are not particularly fond of snails, to a two-year-old however, they are fascinating. She watched their slow progress, calling their fully extended antennae 'ears'. Despite my explanation they remained 'ears', their constant waving causing much giggling.

'They slow,' she commented, as she tilted her head sideways attempting to get a closer look at how the snails actually slithered up the fence. I lifted one off to show her the underneath of the snail and the way it moved. It quickly hid in its shell, she peered intently attempting to discover where it had gone.

There were more giggles when I placed it back on the fence and the snail emerged from its shell continuing its journey.

Creator God, thank you for slowing my steps to a child's pace, for opening my eyes to the wonder of a simple garden snail slithering up a fence. In my adult busyness I rarely take the time to be still and watch, as a child watches. Rarely allow my mind to divert from the jobs I must attend to, to be still and wonder, as a child wonders.

'Let the children come unto me' – in my grown-up-ness I've forgotten you beckon me to kneel at your feet not as a grownup but as a child.

Amen

In Our Backyard

Despite having a dog, we have an immense variety of birds visiting our garden, many using the bird bath outside our kitchen window.

One afternoon I saw two mynahs chatting beneath a rose bush close to the bird bath. One flew to the edge, peering around before jumping into the water and frolicking as only birds can. The second mynah kept up a constant gentle chatter as it jumped around in all directions beneath the rose bush. It appeared to be the look out.

The first mynah, having finished its ablutions, fluttered a water laden flutter to the edge of the bird bath, flapping its wings wildly, before jumping to the protection of the rose bush. The second bird then enjoyed its turn, while the first one, now acting as look out, kept up the same constant gentle chatter.

Eventually, both birds were beneath the rose bush, conversing and preening their feathers, before flying away.

God of our creation, thank you, for creating time and space for me to witness the wonder of your creations. For opening my eyes to an ordinary little bird, reminiscent of the Biblical sparrow, of little financial value. In the ordinariness of my own backyard, watching ordinary little birds, on an ordinary day, I sense your wondrous presence, 'Yet not one sparrow falls to the ground without your ... consent'. (Matthew 10: 29b) I give thanks for my ordinariness and my ordinary days lived in your presence, Creator God.

                                                  Amen

Christmas Is Coming

Santa's chair is ready at the local shops. Christmas goods have been on the shelves for well over a month.

In two weeks, Advent commences, a time of anticipation, awaiting the coming of Jesus. Yet, it is Mary, human Mary, who captures my attention.

She is tired and awkward, hand at her back attempting to ease the pain common in the final weeks of pregnancy. Sitting down is difficult, getting up no easier. Her swollen feet hurt. A first-time mum, each step of the nine-month journey a new experience filled with hope and anticipation, tinged with anxiety at the coming labour. Heavily pregnant Mary is also anxious about the trip to Bethlehem. Like any pregnant woman with five weeks to go Mary wishes it was all over. Like any pregnant woman she hopes she goes full term for the wellbeing of her unborn child.

As we await the retelling of a familiar story, Mary waits for the unfamiliar, the unknown. The New Testament readings tell us little about how Mary felt after the birth of Jesus, except 'Mary remembered all these things and thought deeply about them.' As we approach Advent, may we see the miracle, the fulfilment of a promise, the wonder and hope of Jesus' birth through Mary's eyes, and may we, like Mary, remember all these things as though they are new, and think deeply about them.

The Challenge of The Stable

Advent is not a repeat performance, rather a challenge to enter the stable for the first time. Glossy Christmas cards depict Mary gazing serenely at a sleeping baby Jesus. Joseph hovers protectively. The anxiety of searching for a room has been airbrushed from his demeanour, as has travel dust and childbirth exhaustion from Mary's face. Cardboardy smells of packaged Christmas cards, mask earthy odours of animals confined to a stable.

We've sanitised the stable. Created a safe perspective from which to view Christ's birth.

Yet, the power of the stable message is in its very ordinariness. Without knowing how the story ends, Mary and Joseph place their faith and trust in God. They didn't ask to be chosen. God chose. They obeyed. I'm sure there was dialogue. 'Why me? I'm just an ordinary person! I'm not strong enough! I don't know enough!' God listened, affirmed the choice. Mary and Joseph trusted and obeyed, their transient stable stopover a part of their unknown journey of faith, trust, and obedience.

Advent reminds us not only of Christ's birth, but God's earthly work yet to be fulfilled. It is our transient stopover as we gaze in wonder at the power of God's relationship with the ordinary person to fulfil his promises. I feel the power of God's relationship with Mary and Joseph, a sense of renewal in the stable ordinariness, but struggle with the challenge. Dare I, step through the open stable door on an unknown journey of faith, trust and obedience?

Let Us Make a Joyful Noise

Music may reduce us to tears or make us shout with joy. It may soothe or agitate, inspire or disturb. We add words to music, singing at weddings and funerals, baptisms and confirmations and during the liturgical seasons of the year. Sometimes we sing unaccompanied, our voices creating the music. Other times, music speaks to us in a way words cannot.

Gladys was confined to bed, with advanced dementia, her legs and arms constantly jerking and moving. Nevertheless, she was wheeled to the activities area, joining the other residents of the aged care facility, for their annual Christmas concert. The second the music started, her erratic movements ceased, her frail hands instantly clapping in time to the music. It was a joy to behold. God's voice reaches us through music when nothing else will penetrate the fog.

'Oh come, let us sing to the Lord, let us make a joyful noise to the rock of our salvation.' Ps. 95:10

A New Commandment

'And now I give you a new commandment: love one another. As I have loved you, so you must love one another. If you have love for one another, then everyone will know that you are my disciples.' (John 13: 34-35)

Loving God, the horrors of the Boston bombings are still making headlines, rekindling the terror of September 11. We remember the human sacrifice of war on Anzac Day, the inhumanity of the holocaust is unimaginable for many of us, as is the degradation and cruelty of some regimes in countries far from our own, yet their stories are true.

In a world where hatred, despair, fear and horror seem to be the overriding emotions, where injustice seems to be the norm rather than the exception, where we ourselves are angry at what our fellow human beings are choosing to inflict on the innocent, where we very often feel powerless to not only right the wrongs, but to love one another – the victims and the perpetrators – as you have loved us.

Open our eyes, loving God, give us a little shake. 'Love one another' you commanded us, 'as I have loved you'. You understand our deepest emotions, our sense of powerlessness. Yet you still love us. Teach us to accept our humanness, in doing so we are reminded of our deep need to be loved, not judged, despite our weaknesses.

'Darkness cannot drive out darkness, only light can do that. Hate cannot drive out hate, only love can do that.' – Martin Luther King.

Give us the strength Lord, to light the candle of love, even when our hands tremble with fear and our eyes struggle to see in the dark.

Amen

(This reflection was written soon after the Boston bombings, but its relevancy has not faded.)

Finding Time for Just God and Me

whisper through my busyness, God of my solitude
lead me gently by the hand to a place where time does not tick
where day is wrapped in gentle light and night a kindly dark of sweet sleep
where sounds fall feather-soft, yet your voice is clear
where moss is soft beneath my feet and soothes my knees as I kneel
where the rhythm of day and night restores my breathing to the rhythm of work and sleep
once nourished, God of my solitude
lead me gently by the hand
back to the place of my busyness
that my busyness may reflect the purpose you have planned for me

                                                  Amen

About the Author

Judith A Green grew up on a wheat and sheep farm outside Warracknabeal. The cycle of the seasons her calendar as were the times of abundant crops and the dust of drought.

A love of books, of reading and the telling of family stories nurtured her in her early years, as was a sense of belonging to a faith and a broader community.

Her career beyond her school days was as a kindergarten teacher when she delighted in planning experiences to nurture active imaginations. Judith believes this creates the desire to explore, to being open to the excitement of discovery, the magic and wonder of learning.

From her early teens Judith has explored her connection to people and place through poetry, short stories, and non-fiction articles. Her work is influenced by a keen interest in family history, history in general, but particularly Australian history and the stories told by our First Nations people.

Judith has been placed or Commended in a variety of competitions and published in several anthologies, the most recent being the annual Society of Women Writers Victoria journal *Sparx*.

In 2020 Judith's first book length work *Inherited Touch*, exploring the resilience of her female forebears, was released.

www.ingramcontent.com/pod-product-compliance
Lightning Source LLC
Chambersburg PA
CBHW071743080526
44588CB00013B/2135